Negotiating for Success

Rowmark

Easy Step by Step Guide

Negotiating for Success

Brian Lomas

Rowmark

Published by Rowmark Limited
65 Rogers Mead
Hayling Island
Hampshire
PO11 0PL
ISBN 0954804546

Edited and typeset by
Frances Hackeson Freelance Publishing Services, Brinscall, Lancs
Printed in Great Britain by
RPM Reprographics Ltd, Chichester

For Mark

Contents

Contents

Contents

About the author

This is the fourth Easy Step by Step Guide written by Brian Lomas – so you'll be forgiven for thinking he has made a career out of it. But no – he is a trainer, consultant, mentor, coach, lecturer *and* an author.

So with such a packed schedule, why has Rowmark asked him to write another guide? Well the short answer is that his guides sell!

The long answer is that his writing is based on many years of practical knowledge and experience of working (and living) in the UK and USA. It is that knowledge which makes his writing actually capable of making a difference to you, the reader, because it avoids getting stuck in theoretical analysis or idealistic fancy.

This guide – along with all the others in the series – is about giving you hints, tips and techniques that you can use in everyday situations. And Brian, the author, has proven adept at achieving this in his writing – but read on and judge that for yourself.

Introduction

When you embark on a negotiation, you seek to achieve a certain outcome. So there should be a single 'best' way to negotiate – right? Well no, not necessarily – as this guide will show.

Let me illustrate what I mean here with just two options:

Option one: I go on holiday and visit an antique market. The likelihood that I will ever meet the stallholder again is remote. So when I see something I want to buy, I want it as cheap as possible. I don't care what the stallholder thinks of me as long as I get it cheap. The stallholder might dislike my tough 'take-it-or-leave-it' stance, but if he sells it to me cheaply, I am delighted and the negotiation is complete.

Option two: Another antique market, another stallholder – but this time one I visit regularly. It's likely that the stallholder will have something in the future I want to buy. If I used the above style, he or she probably would remember my toughness and decide not to sell to me again. So I have to negotiate differently.

I still want a good price but this time I also want us both to feel good about it during and after the negotiation. That way, if we negotiate in the future, neither of us will be wary of striking the deal. So toughness is out – this time, both the price and the relationship have to be successfully negotiated.

Which is best? The answer is 'it depends' and what it might depend upon is explored in this guide. Then you can decide for yourself which style to use when.

How to use this guide

Your choice – open to a page and read the 'boxed' text for key points, read the summaries at the end of a chapter to gain a sense of what each is about, check the contents list for a specific issue or just read from cover to cover.

Whatever your approach, I give you one suggestion before starting:

> Think of past negotiations you don't regard as a 'success'.
>
> As you read, think about what would have made them more successful.

What you will learn from this guide

• how different approaches can have different

impacts – especially for the future

- how to plan for a negotiation
- how fulfilling the role of customer or supplier can impact your approach to a negotiation
- how to prioritize needs, wants and success criteria
- how to avoid a 'bottom line' without surrendering key points
- how to work within and around authority levels
- how to determine the right time and place for a negotiation
- how to adopt the most successful style for a specific negotiation
- how body language and tone of voice can have a direct impact on negotiations
- how to build relationships, rapport and trust in negotiations
- how to motivate people to start, continue and complete a negotiation
- how to respond to tactics and consider whether or not their use is appropriate
- how to run a negotiation – from start to finish – and ensure clarity of understanding
- how to close a deal and hold people to the agreement.
- how to check you are fully prepared for success.

1
Negotiation – what is it?

This should be easy – let's try:

> A negotiation is a communication which results in an exchange between two or more parties.

We will challenge this, however, because it describes a *successful* negotiation (an exchange actually takes place). Negotiations might never result in an exchange – perhaps when the parties agree to walk away from a discussion. So we need to try again:

> A negotiation is a communication in which the parties seek agreement to an exchange between them.

This looks good – we'll work on this as a starter.

Opportunities to negotiate

We negotiate all the time – in fact:

> Rarely will a day pass without you being involved in some form of negotiation.

Some examples of when you negotiate in business:

- setting/agreeing targets and/or pay and benefits
- seeking co-operation from others within your own organization
- forming partnerships with organizations, trade unions, government
- influencing people to prioritize in accord with your wishes/needs
- seeking to pass work on to someone
- dealings with external suppliers, service providers and customers – on timescales, prices, quality, terms and conditions etc
- settling disputes with customers, suppliers or internally.

And on the personal front, you negotiate when:

- buying or selling homes, cars or whatever
- forming or breaking relationships
- dividing responsibilities or tasks amongst your friends and/or family

- seeking to persuade others to a particular course of action
- deciding where to go for a night out!

Mutual benefits from a negotiation

The principle underlying all negotiations is that each party gets something (from the exchange) that they would not otherwise have.

I negotiate to buy a car. The seller gets my money, I get the car. Without the negotiation, neither of us would have what we seek. The benefit I will derive from owning the car will be very different from the benefit that they derive from the money – but we both benefit from the negotiation. We can say, therefore, that:

> A negotiation aims to deliver benefit to each party through the agreed exchange.

So is it still a negotiation if one or more of the negotiators gets 'nothing' in exchange? Let's take two examples:

1 I negotiate with you to paint my house for free. My benefit is clear – a painted house. But would you also benefit? Possibly – you might get great satisfaction and/or enjoyment from the work. So we might have an agreed exchange, even though I may not agree to paint your house on the same basis.

2 I agree to hand over my money to a mugger in

'exchange' for not causing me physical harm. The mugger benefits from my money and I suppose I benefit from remaining uninjured.

Can we really accept these two examples as negotiated agreements? Well:

> There is no presumption in our definition of a negotiation that it is either 'fair' or delivers 'happiness' – merely that there is an agreed exchange.

And in each example, each party agreed to get *something* out of it – so they are negotiations. But it does lead to another factor about negotiations:

Negotiating the 'lesser of two evils'

Ask anyone who has sold their home and been faced with a last-minute demand from the buyer: 'Reduce the price or the deal is off!' Is this fair? Would we be happy? Probably not – but we might still agree to the sale at a reduced price as it is a lesser 'evil' than losing the sale altogether.

In business, a trade union might be negotiating for a pay rise. The employers want higher productivity and/ or a reduction in the size of the workforce. The union may not like what the employer is asking for in exchange for more pay, but it wouldn't stop them seeking the best possible outcome.

So:

> In reality, negotiating between the lesser of two evils happens all the time.

Negotiating for success

It's time now to consider what we mean by the title of this guide: Negotiating *for Success.*

When selling my home, I want the highest possible price – the buyer wants the lowest. So our criteria for what will make this negotiation a 'success' is different.

> Your success will not necessarily deliver success to others and vice versa.

So to negotiate 'successfully', we obviously need to think about the possible success criteria in a negotiation.

Success criteria

Success criteria will be a mix of all or any of the following:

- what you get as a result of the negotiation. (e.g. I sell my house)
- the degree to which you got what you wanted (e.g. how near to my asking price was the final price?)
- how much you have had to give to enable the exchange (did I have to include any carpets and furniture?)

- the degree to which you were prepared to give as much as you have (if I didn't want the carpets and furniture, no problem!)
- how the negotiation's outcome might be assessed with the benefit of hindsight. (Would I look at the negotiation differently if I knew they would have been prepared to pay 5% more?)
- how positive you feel before, during and after the negotiation. (Was I happy with the sale or did the buyer make it tortuous?)
- the impact that the negotiation and its outcome has on the relationship between the parties. (Will I ever speak to my buyers again?)
- how costly in terms of time and money has the negotiation been? How efficiently was it concluded? (Did the sale go smoothly or were there arguments that increased my lawyer's charges?)
- to what degree do the other parties achieve their success criteria? (Are the buyers happy?)
- that the agreed exchange actually takes place. (Did we complete the sale?)

And potentially:

- if you walk away from an agreement, was it the right thing to do?

Identifying your own success criteria is a key starting point for all negotiations – otherwise how else would you know whether or not your negotiation is a success?

> Know your own success criteria before you start negotiating.

And not all of our criteria will be equally important:

> **Place all your success criteria in order of importance.**

For example: I might be far more interested in getting a high selling price for my house than whether or not I feel comfortable about talking with the buyer in the future.

The other parties' success criteria

If you want the other parties to regard a negotiation as a success you will need to deliver some (if not all) of their criteria. Even if you don't want the other party to achieve success, knowing their criteria will help you understand their conduct during a negotiation. So:

> **Seek to ascertain the success criteria for each negotiating party – if not in advance, then as early as you can in any communication.**

An advantage to delivering at least some of the other party's success criteria is that it will substantially increase their commitment to follow it through rather than seek a way out.

Common success criteria

Some criteria between the parties will be common – in our house sale example, we both want to move house. This perspective can be invaluable:

> If negotiations get 'difficult', discussing common success criteria will help to move the communication forward.

Conflicting success criteria

This is a reality. For example: in our house selling example, one wants to sell at the highest price, the other to buy it at the lowest. It is this conflict which embodies what needs to be negotiated.

Changing success criteria

We should bear in mind that:

> What a negotiator regards as a success in one negotiation does not necessarily apply in another.

Nor can we assume that success criteria are fixed during a negotiation.

> During a negotiation, parties can – and do – change their criteria for success and/ or their relative importance.

To continue with our example:

In negotiating the sale of my first home, my main criteria for success might be to get as much money as possible. When I sell my next house, the timing of the sale might actually be more important than a small price change. But if something happens during the second sale to change that priority I might decide to place timing below that of sale price.

And the same runs true in business negotiations. An employer might seek an improvement in productivity in the first round of pay negotiations but in a later one seek to change the employees' working hours. They then might seek to change the working hours as a top priority for something else during that negotiation – perhaps reduced overtime rates. So:

There is a significant risk that anyone might change their success criteria between or during negotiations.

And managing these risks is what this guide is all about to enable your negotiations to be a success.

In summary

- a negotiation is a communication in which the parties seek agreement to an exchange between them

- negotiations take place all the time both at work and at home

- negotiations are about each party getting a benefit from the exchange – even if it is the choice between the lesser of two evils
- people will have different success criteria for each negotiation they join
- different parties to the same negotiation will have different success criteria
- know your success criteria and their relative importance before starting a negotiation
- seek early identification of the success criteria and their relative importance for all parties in a negotiation
- fulfilling the success criteria of the negotiating parties will increase the level of commitment amongst everyone to implement the agreement
- any common ground of success criteria is always useful if the negotiation becomes 'difficult'
- the negotiation will centre on any conflicting success criteria
- people's success criteria may change during a negotiation.

2

What can be negotiated?

Well, just about anything can be a **negotiable**:

> A negotiable is anything which might be exchanged during a negotiation.

And there are two basic types of negotiable – the **tangible** and the **emotional**.

Tangible negotiables

These are easily identified. For example: when negotiating the sale of a house, the tangibles include the house itself, a diary date for moving, a price, the contents which are to be included in the sale etc.

Tangibles will be typically documented and quantified in some way. So, when selling a house, the following will be agreed in writing:

- the address and defined boundary of the specific property under negotiation

- a specific date on which the price will be paid and the house will be made available to the buyer

- a specific purchase price

- a list of specific contents included or perhaps excluded from the agreement. For example: when selling a house, the garden plants are generally regarded as included – unless the vendor specifies otherwise. So when I last sold, I had to list all the plants I wanted to take with me and exclude them from the sale.

When negotiating, we typically remember most of the tangible negotiables – but note:

> **Failing to document tangible *specifics* can cause significant problems.**

For instance: imagine the response if it was never documented when a negotiated pay increase was to be implemented!

Tangible needs and wants

Tangible negotiables can be sub-divided into 'wants and needs'. Two examples:

1 When selling my home, I might *want* to get twice (or three times) what it is worth. A would-be buyer might *want* it at half the market value.

2 In business, when employers and employees are

engaged in pay negotiations – the former (generally) doesn't *want* to pay as much as the latter *wants* to receive.

In the above examples, the wants are in conflict and there is no way forward for the parties:

> Sticking to tangible *wants* gives no room for negotiating.

But there is an alternative. Let's re-consider the two examples:

1 When I sell my house, I might *need* enough money from the sale to buy another. A buyer *needs* to be able to afford it.

2 When seeking to agree a pay increase from an employer, the employees might *need* to be given their market worth and the employer *needs* to keep them on the payroll and motivated.

Both of these examples provide room for manoeuvre in a negotiation, not least because 'needs' are (typically) more reasonable than 'wants' and there are different ways to achieve success. To illustrate:

1 If I *want* twice the market value of my house, the chances of a sale are negligible. But if the buyer can enable me to buy another home, there will be lots of homes from which my *needs* can be met.

2 If I *want* a 20% pay increase, the employer could refuse and we are at an impasse. But if I state my *need* is to reflect my market worth, there could be a mix of options negotiated – enhance my pension, reduce my hours and/or give me a pay increase.

So:

> **Stating tangible *needs* is a basis for negotiating.**

Emotional negotiables

Every negotiation involves emotions and they can have a profound impact on the progress towards an agreement by causing us to act subjectively and frequently irrationally. However, they are not necessarily that easy to identify. Let's illustrate this with our house selling example:

- The buyer may fall in love with the house. They may be (emotionally) pressured by their family or friends to make the move and/or buy this specific house. Yet they are unlikely to let the seller know of such pressure for fear that the seller might take advantage and increase their asking price.

- The seller might be selling because they need the proceeds to buy urgent medical treatment for a loved one. Again, the seller's reluctance to reveal this might be caused by fear that it will give the upper hand to the buyer.

Therefore:

> **Rarely will all the emotions be revealed in a negotiation.**

Emotional negotiables are also present in business

negotiations. Consider:

- the senior manager who is driven by an emotional need 'to be seen' as successful.
- the person who gets upset when they think their needs are being disregarded or disrespected
- when a negotiation falters because one party insults another.

So:

> **Always take account of the emotions in a negotiation.**

Emotional needs and wants

Does the principle of stating tangible needs rather than wants work with emotional negotiables? Alas, no!

Let's look at a business example. I negotiate the best possible deal for my organization, but believe that it is not quite good enough to avoid me 'losing face' amongst my peers. If I emotionally *want* to look good in front of my peers, I might choose to scupper the deal rather than proceed with it.

Rationally, we would say that such action would be wrong. But who said emotions were rational? Before you discard this, ask yourself:

> **Have I ever let my heart rule my head?**

If your answer to the question above is 'yes', then:

> When negotiating, address the emotional needs *and* wants as well as the tangible needs to deliver success.

In summary

- a negotiable is anything which might be exchanged during a negotiation
- any agreement regarding tangible negotiables should be documented and very specific
- sticking to tangible wants gives no room for negotiating, but discussing tangible needs does
- emotional negotiables are present in every negotiation
- emotions can cause subjective and irrational behaviour and yet the reasons for that behaviour will rarely be identified
- intangible needs *and* wants have to be addressed in some way to deliver success.

3

The different parties

In this chapter, we will look at the different parties to a negotiation.

> A negotiation is not restricted to a communication between just two parties.

For instance: a trade union, employer, employees and potentially the government could be involved in a high profile pay negotiation.

The Negotiators

Before starting a negotiation, find out:

- the names/roles of the people with whom you will be negotiating

- whom or what does each party seek to represent in that negotiation? For example: a human resources negotiator might represent a company as a union represents the workers.
- any relevant background from past negotiations
- the (probable) success criteria for each party to the negotiation – the tangibles and the emotions
- the authority level each party has in concluding a negotiation. Negotiations do take place between people who do not have the authority to enforce an agreement. For instance: in the negotiations over the EU constitution in 2005, the final say rested for many countries on winning a national referendum. Such scenarios are perhaps not ideal for the negotiators – but a reality nonetheless. However, there is more to consider here.

When authority is outside of the negotiation

When authority is held outside of the negotiation, consider:

Is an external authority merely a tactic?

Sometimes negotiators want to avoid being 'put on the spot' or are nervous that they may be panicked or pressured into an agreement they might later wish to reconsider. So they create an external authority to provide that 'escape-clause'. However:

> There could be valid reasons for introducing an external authority.

Perhaps external authority is needed to sanction the efforts of someone 'learning' to negotiate or because those in authority do not have the time to go through all the necessary detail.

Successful negotiations can be undertaken with external authorities, providing:

> The success criteria of external authorities are established before or in the early stages of the negotiation.

So when democratic governments come together to negotiate a treaty, aides will start the negotiation process before government ministers finish it. These ministers, however, will (or, at least, should) consider what their constituents want and/or need from any treaty before signing it.

Negotiators and the 'experts'

An 'expert' might be introduced during or at the end of making an agreement. These people can typically stall, but not stop, a negotiation. For instance:

A lawyer might stall negotiations over buying a house by raising legal concerns. The lawyers, however, have no authority to walk away from the negotiation – only the parties they represent can do that.

Experts can be used for positive reasons – perhaps to discuss highly technical issues for which the negotiators don't have the necessary understanding or knowledge. Preferably expert involvement would be agreed at the outset of a negotiation, but as long as they are introduced before negotiations are concluded, it is manageable. But sometimes:

> **Experts can be introduced unexpectedly.**

Let's say a customer agrees to have a custom-made luxury yacht designed and built. The fixed price deal is signed and then – but only then – the customer introduces an engineering crew to review the yacht's manoeuvrability. They might then ask for changes to the specification, which might wipe out the yacht-builder's profit.

On such a fixed price contract, the experts have been introduced too late in the negotiation. Had it been known – and publicized – in advance that these experts were being involved, caveats could have been entered into the fixed price contract for a re-negotiation should it be proven necessary.

There is one more aspect to consider about the introduction of an expert:

> **Is the use of an expert a tactic?**

Occasionally, an agreement will be made subject 'to contract' or 'agreed terms and conditions' which are drawn up by experts not involved in the negotiation.

There's nothing inherently wrong here – but it can be abused:

Detail drawn up by experts can hold surprises!

Consider:

- how many times have you been referred to the small print of a contract you signed but never read?

- how many times you have read and understood the small print before signing an agreement?

- have you ever made a purchase only to be told afterwards that there are extra charges to pay?

How can we sum up the role of experts in a negotiation then?

Value experts but beware of them!

Negotiators impact other people

Rarely will a negotiation only impact the people actually negotiating:

- a trade union represents their members

- a pressure group negotiates on behalf of the beliefs of many members

- politicians negotiate on behalf of the people who elect them

- lawyers, accountants and agents negotiate for their clients.

Now, the question arises:

> **How well do negotiators understand the needs and wants of those they represent?**

If this was never in doubt, why would an employer occasionally seek to bypass the union and go straight to the workforce with a proposal? And to demonstrate a complete understanding of the needs and wants of its members, a union might ballot its members to solicit their support and thereby strengthen its own position in the negotiations.

Without the support of those represented, any negotiation is next to useless. So negotiators must:

> **Be mindful of the needs and wants of the people represented and impacted by any agreement.**

Yet do not forget that:

> **Representative negotiators will still have emotional needs and wants of their own.**

So a negotiation might collapse simply because one party insults another and refuses to apologize.

The impact of publicity

> **Negotiable wants can, as a result of publicity, become negotiable needs**

For instance: In a high profile pay negotiation, an employer might say to the media that they do not *want* to pay more than an extra 3%. The union might publicize that they *want* 6%.

Those represented by the negotiators take up these publicized figures, repeat them and make them something they *need* as part of the eventual agreement. How many times have you heard union members *demanding* the percentage pay increase asked for by their representatives? And employer groups insisting there is no more money for pay increases than that stated in the media? In other words, a negotiated *want* has become a *need*. So:

> **Agree to keep the negotiations 'behind closed doors' until an agreement is reached.**

Negotiating with a team

Picture the scene: A supplier goes to negotiate with a customer's organization and comes face to face with a panel of eight people!

Now this shouldn't happen because we have already advocated that you should know who you are going to negotiate with before you start. If you then believed it necessary, you might also take along a panel of eight negotiators.

But why have a panel of negotiators? There are a number of possible reasons:

- no single negotiator has complete knowledge or understanding of that to be negotiated
- such is the importance of a negotiation, that no single person can be trusted with the responsibility
- there is a general lack of trust amongst the negotiating panel
- there is a lack of trust in the other party
- 'two heads are better than one' – but eight?
- tactics – some panel members might play the bully and others an accommodating style in the belief that it will maximize the benefit they get from the negotiation.

If you are faced with a panel, remember that:

> Each member of the panel might have their own needs and wants – and they may be in conflict.

Negotiating as a team

Should you decide on team negotiating, call a team meeting before the negotiations start and:

- explain/clarify why a team is required
- understand everyone's needs and wants. This may

involve an internal negotiation!

- identify roles and responsibilities during the discussions, including that of a chairperson

- determine how any disagreements within the team will be dealt with away from the other negotiating parties

- plan how any team member should respond if approached individually by one of the other parties. Such approaches might be deliberate or accidental and can be highly detrimental – especially if one panel member is quoted as saying something which is a complete surprise to the rest of their team.

- emphasize that no one has the sole authority to make the agreement. (This necessitates adjournments for the team to discuss progress among themselves.)

Mediators and arbitrators

If negotiations stall, the parties can bring in a mediator or an arbitrator.

- a mediator meets with all the parties to seek an agreed way through the impasse. The negotiating parties still have the final say in whether or not there is to be an agreement.

- An arbitrator meets with each party in turn and imposes an agreement on all the parties that they deem fair and equitable. Here, the negotiating parties 'sign over' their rights to agree or disagree with the negotiated outcome.

Styles of negotiating

There are three basic styles of negotiating – being tough, being a pushover and being a collaborator.

We will explore each of these three styles over the following chapters, but one of the key characteristics that must be identified now is that:

> **Each style employs its own tactics.**

And such tactics will be dealt with 'en masse' in chapter 8.

In summary

- a negotiation can involve more than two parties
- find out as much as you can about the people with whom you will be negotiating and what they need and want – before you start
- determine the wants and needs of any authority or expert external to the negotiation and why such roles are required
- subject 'to contract' or 'agreed terms and conditions' can hold surprises
- a negotiation frequently impacts people not party to the negotiation – but their wants and needs must still be appreciated
- negotiators have needs and wants of their own

over and above what they seek to negotiate on behalf of others

- it is risky to publicize progress in a negotiation until the agreement is actually made

- if faced with a negotiating panel, consider the reasons for this as well as the needs and wants of each panel member

- if negotiating as part of a team, prepare thoroughly before starting the negotiation

- if negotiations stall, consider using a mediator or arbitrator

- there are three basic styles of negotiator: the 'tough', the 'pushover' and the 'collaborator' – each employing their own tactics.

4

The 'tough' negotiator

Some of you might be intimidated by this style, others excited by it.

Let's start by describing what we mean by 'tough':

Their beliefs, goals and success criteria

Tough negotiators are somewhat egotistic in that they believe that they know best. They have their own view of what is fair, what is right, and thus seek to impose their ideas and will on others. The irony is that they don't always know that they are acting in this way – it can be just the way they are as people.

> 'Tough' can be a pseudonym for an intimidating bully.

Their goal is:

> **Tough negotiators must win and the others must lose.**

Their success criteria will be to gain as much and as many of their tangible and emotional needs and wants as possible, exchanging the absolute minimum in return. They care little for what others think of them.

Their cultural fit

This is straightforward:

> **They disregard others' cultural needs – unless, that is, it serves their purpose.**

Their words and voice

This person is not always courteous or polite – quite the opposite in fact. So don't expect too many words like 'please' or 'thank you' – and don't be surprised if a few swear words creep in to the discussion.

Their favourite words are: 'I want', 'I need', 'I expect', 'I demand ...'

It is likely that they will seek to undermine others, typically stereotyping or patronizing them: 'You junior managers need to listen to your betters ...'

Their voice will be forceful, threatening, perhaps shouting and often the loudest voice in the room. It could also be a very deliberate and authoritative tone and pace of voice.

Their body language

There is an important caveat here to *all body language* application and interpretation mentioned in this guide:

> **Body language differs widely between cultures and nationalities.**
>
> **Be sensitive to these differences.**

So how might the tough negotiator act?

Well, their theme of intimidation can carry through to their body language in all sorts of ways from overt to the most subtle of application. They are, however, unlikely to use all the following behaviours at the same time:

- We each need physical space – how much space depends on our relationships, our working environment and our culture. So you would 'allow' someone you care about to get physically closer to you than a total stranger – just as you would in a noisy environment, so you can hear each other speak. A tough negotiator, however, abuses and invades others' personal space without permission or cause.

- They aim for their eye level to be the higher, forcing

others to literally 'look up' to them. The exception here is if they seek to show their 'authority' in a different way – perhaps being the only person sitting, or using a larger and more comfortable chair.

- If choosing a seat round a table, they would select either the one opposite the other party (confrontation) or at the head of the table ('I'm in charge here').

- When others are talking, tough negotiators are quite likely to look away (showing disinterest), fidget, shake their head or somehow show exacerbation at their comments – perhaps by rolling their eyes.

- Tough negotiators might point their finger, lean forward, stare or threaten.

Their tactics

There are many potential tactics that tough negotiators might use – consciously or otherwise:

- dishonesty. Yes, they lie!

- withholding information and/or knowledge

- power plays – 'I know your boss personally'. (This could be true – but it may not be.)

- quoting third parties or sources. They might quote an obscure law, trusting it will not be checked. Such quotes may be inaccurate

- seeking a higher authority (thus demeaning yours) – 'if you can't agree, then I'll take it to someone who can'

- stubbornness (repeating their demands in the belief that you will give in)
- claiming reasonableness (when they are not being so)
- refusing to listen
- refusing to let others speak
- refusing to speak
- moving the goalposts – if they aren't succeeding, they might approach it from a different angle (but have the same agenda)
- demanding a concession at the last minute which could change the 'balance' of an agreement
- threats and bluffs
- shuffling or packing away their papers to suggest they are giving up (in the face of your 'unreasonableness')
- abruptly ending negotiations (hanging up the telephone, storming out of meetings etc).

> **How you respond to each tactic will depend on the style of negotiating you wish to adopt.**

We will discuss how to respond to these tactics in chapter 8.

The upside ... and the downside

Tough negotiators are singularly focused to win – to get what they need and want. They may well be seen

– especially in the short term – as highly successful by their peers and the organization they represent.

Their preparation time is limited because they will only put their effort into researching their own needs and wants, which they have no need to prioritize (because they want it all). The only research undertaken in respect of the other parties will be to identify their weaknesses. They aim to complete negotiations relatively fast.

The downside includes:

• an agreement may never be reached – especially if two 'tough' negotiators come face to face

• the basis of the negotiation will probably be on inflated demands, making it difficult to move them to a point of 'reasonableness'

• any agreement may stall on implementation because any other party will see little benefit in 'doing their bit'

• their ability to encourage the parties back to the negotiating table in the future is severely diminished.

When is tough appropriate?

> Despite the downside, there can be times when toughness is appropriate.

Consider which of these scenarios would warrant being 'tough':

• governments threatening war as being the only

way to secure ultimate peace

- a tough managerial style being the only way to avoid bankruptcy

- parents refusing their child yet another chocolate bar, despite the threat of tears and tantrums

- at a market, arguing until a price is as low as possible irrespective of what others think.

And if you disagree with all of the above examples:

> Can you honestly not think of a single occasion when being tough is the right thing to do?

In summary

- tough negotiators believe they know best and will seek to impose their beliefs on others

- tough negotiators don't always see themselves as tough

- their goal is that they must win and others must lose

- their objective is to get as much as they can in exchange for as little as possible, having disregard for the needs and wants of others

- they will disregard culture unless it serves their goal

- body language is worth noting but remember it

differs widely between different cultures

- their words, voice and body language will give indications of their style

- they can employ a wide range of tactics – consciously or otherwise

- there is an upside and downside to this style and there will be times when it is appropriate.

5

The 'pushover' negotiator

Now if you were uncertain how you felt about being 'tough', you are probably saying that one should never be a 'pushover'. Well let's see ...

Their beliefs, goals and success criteria

The pushover negotiator will believe that friendship and a good (or at least calm) relationship are more valuable than the deal itself. Some might therefore describe these people as 'nice', having real discomfort with conflict which they will actively seek to avoid. They are trusting of others and will need considerable evidence to believe otherwise.

They are likely to be resigned to getting little of their wants and needs – they may not even ask, let alone persist, in trying to secure them, because, they believe, others' needs and wants take precedence. They would consider themselves lucky to achieve their 'bottom-line'.

The outcome:

> The other party gets what they want and need – they will win.
>
> Inherently, that means I will lose.

Their cultural fit

Here they would try to do 'the right thing' by seeking to adapt to others' culture, even at the expense of their own. This is not to say they will not make cultural mistakes – just they would be unintentional and, when discovered, prompt profound apologies.

Their words and voice

They don't usually say a lot! The words they might use are apologetic, deferential and concessionary: 'I'm sorry to interrupt you – you must be busy ...' or 'Whatever you think is best'.

Their voice will be quiet, softly spoken and possibly faltering.

Their body language

Let's consider some of the possible body language of the 'pushover' negotiator:

- personal space differs according to how well they know the other party – they might get physically close to someone they feel emotionally comfortable with but keep strangers at a distance

- they are unlikely to make much eye contact or look directly at others
- they are quite likely to let others choose their seat first and then accept being told where to sit. They would seek to avoid the 'head of the table'.
- they do listen – to discover whether or not the other parties are happy – but may not necessarily understand (nor ask for clarification)
- pushover negotiators typically show some form of discomfort or lack of confidence in their body language.

Their tactics

Since they tend to follow where others lead their tactics tend to be re-active rather than proactive. Their range of available tactics is limited, therefore, but would include:

- silence and/or play on their naivety. This is their most natural tactic and can, on occasion, reveal some information from the other parties which might otherwise remain hidden
- lack of honesty (in that they will not communicate what they truly need and want for fear of upsetting someone)
- appealing to the other's better nature – if they have one!
- the sob story – the tears – the apologies – the begging
- inflating the importance of anything that helps them 'save face'.

Again, we will consider later the most appropriate way of responding to such tactics.

The upside ... and the downside

These people will be regarded by many as 'good' people. Others will get what they need and want and thus be happy to negotiate with them again in the future. The negotiation itself will be unlikely to negatively escalate, because the relationship is all important.

Sometimes it can pay in the long term – pushovers earn 'favours' by their style and it may be reciprocated in the future (but there is no guarantee).

Ironically their style also can have an intimidating impact on others. Since a pushover might seek to avoid a negotiation, it can make a tough deadline even more difficult to achieve. As a result, they might get all sorts of concessions without even turning up to the negotiation!

On the downside:

- the pushover typically gets little – if anything – of what they actually need and want

- others might look down on them or take advantage and could therefore be greedy in their demands – knowing the pushovers will concede

- others can get impatient or frustrated at the pushover for not saying what they want or mean

- the pushover's lack of confidence and/or self-esteem is likely to be re-enforced by each negotiation – making it harder for them in the future.

When is being a pushover appropriate?

So all this might make you think that being a pushover is never appropriate. Well what about:

- would a government ever seek a negotiated agreement to a border dispute by conceding territory to avoid a war?

- in business, would a manufacturer ever agree to take on a loss-making contract merely to keep the workforce occupied?

- would a retailer ever sell anything as a loss-leader in the hope of attracting customers into their stores?

- would you ever respond to a need or want from a loved one even though you have neither the time nor the money?

So there will be occasions when being a pushover is right – perhaps when it is the lesser of two evils (as with the first three scenarios above) or when the importance of the relationship outweighs anything else (as in the case of loved ones).

In summary

- the 'pushover' negotiator believes that others wants and needs take precedence over their own

- their goal is that others must win therefore they will lose

- their success will be in meeting the needs and wants of others, hoping for something in exchange: preserving the relationship is of paramount importance.

- they will seek to adapt to the culture of the other parties and be very apologetic if they fail in this

- their (few) words, tone of voice and body language will give indications of their style

- their tactics evolve with the style and are therefore frequently unconscious activities

- there is an upside and downside to this style and there may be times it is considered appropriate.

6

The collaborative negotiator

This person seeks all the parties to work together to find the best possible outcome. See what you think about this style of negotiating.

Their beliefs, goals and success criteria

The collaborative negotiator believes that a negotiation is the resolution of a joint problem and, that by being open, honest and respectful, they can fulfil as many of everyone's needs and wants (tangible and emotional) as possible.

They seek to preserve and enhance the relationship between the parties, thus substantially improving the likelihood of its successful implementation. There should be 'no regrets' about the negotiation with the benefit of hindsight and therefore the path to negotiating in the future will be smoothed.

> ## The goal: all parties win.

The collaborator will seek, in the event of there being no agreement, for everyone to be comfortable with that decision.

Their cultural fit

> Collaborators will seek to work within the bounds of others' cultures – but not necessarily without challenge if it contradicts their own.

For instance: religions attach significance to different days of the week, which may restrict when business negotiations can and cannot be undertaken. A collaborator will respect this – but not at the expense of countering his/her own religious beliefs.

Their words and voice

Emphasizing their approach, they will use terms like 'we', 'together', 'mutual benefit', 'how else can we resolve ...', 'what do you think?'. They use questions to discover exactly what is negotiable (and what is not).

Their voice will be calm, confident and deliberate without appearing contrived or unnatural.

Their body language

Collaborators deliberately adopt a more complete set of body language techniques rather than the occasional and disjointed usage discussed in the previous styles.

- collaborators respect others needs for personal space. If there is doubt about what is appropriate, they are more likely to play safe rather than run the risk of offence.

- lots of eye contact – without staring – especially at key points in the discussion

- they will seek to create an equitable and encouraging body language. For instance, their eye level would be neither below the other parties (suggesting a pushover) nor above (reminiscent of tough negotiators). However, they may well, for instance, drop their eye contact below that of someone who has adopted a pushover style, to encourage them to express what they think and feel

- they would not take the head of the table seat, nor one opposite others. They would prefer side-by-side seating or, more likely, at right angles to others. This sends an encouraging, cooperative message and yet still enables easy eye contact

- they tend to listen more than talk because they will have prepared how they will reveal their needs and wants and need to encourage the other party to do the same. They will give speakers lots of encouraging signals to show that they are interested in what is being said

- collaborators show confidence in the manner of

their body language.

Their tactics

- honesty and openness
- questioning to identify and understand the needs and wants of all parties
- respect for others and their opinions even when they don't agree, but challenging unreasonable attitude or behaviour
- staying calm and objective – irrespective of the reactions of others.

These tactics are the means by which they seek to achieve their goal. For responding to tactics, see chapter 8.

The upside ... and the downside

On the upside, the maximum exchange of needs and wants takes place. A good working relationship is established and maintained for the future.

On the downside, this collaborative style perhaps needs more deliberate persistence and patience than the other styles of negotiation. This is especially true when faced with a view that successful negotiations require a winner and a loser.

Potentially, doubts may occur for even the strongest advocate of collaboration: 'Had I been tougher, could I have achieved more?' While it is unlikely that this is the case, it can inhibit their advocacy of this approach in the future.

When is collaboration appropriate?

There are lots of possibilities – here are a few:

- governments sign treaties of cooperation and friendship

- in business, corporations form partnerships with each other – perhaps in joint funding initiatives

- when friends decide to go on holiday together, they seek to meet everyone's needs and wants as well as having a better time than if they went alone.

In summary

- the collaborator believes that everyone's needs and wants are a problem to be resolved within a strong relationship. They seek an exchange of as many needs and wants as possible in an open, honest and respectful manner

- their goal is that both parties should win – a goal that would not change with the benefit of hindsight

- they will balance the cultural needs and wants of all parties

- their words, voice and body language will exude confidence and calmness

- their tactics are inherent within the style of collaboration.

7

The meeting of negotiators

We will now explore what happens when two (or more) negotiators come together, each with their own style and approach.

When tough meets tough

It can be very entertaining to watch – two toughies 'fighting' it out. Typically their demands and tactics will escalate and they will end up getting nowhere!

> Each party will typically claim that an agreement couldn't be reached because of the other's unreasonable demands.

When tough meets pushover

The toughie will 'win' lots and give very little in return. They will have little concern about changing the agreement unilaterally in their favour or seeking to re-negotiate it for an even better deal.

The pushover will be intimidated and is unlikely to express their needs and wants. Their aim will be getting to the end of the negotiation as fast as possible with the least amount of 'pain'.

When tough meets collaborator

Tough negotiators are likely to persist and try multiple tactics to get around the collaborator – personal attacks and claims (wrongly) for reasonableness are high on their agenda.

> Agreement on the first occasion is unlikely. The toughie is likely to walk away to think about new tactics for 'round two'.

The collaborator will believe (correctly) that they are doing most of the work – not least by providing a way for the toughie to return to the negotiation without losing face and managing the multiple manouvres and tactics thrown at them.

The key to what will finally happen here is who has the greatest persistence.

> A persistent collaborator will ensure that everyone will get a substantial amount of their (reasonable) needs and wants.

However, if the collaborator concedes ground to the toughie, the latter will seize on this as a weakness from which it is difficult to recover. The collaborator might then collapse under the verbal battering they receive.

A possibility here is that the parties agree not to agree and the negotiation ends.

When pushover meets pushover

A very pleasant experience – perhaps frustrating, especially for those on the side-lines. Lots of chat and pleasantries!

However, there will be little progress on the negotiation because neither party will disclose too much for fear of causing offence.

> So the likelihood here is either a very basic agreement or frequent deferment to discuss it further.

When pushover meets collaborator

Since the spirit of the collaborator is that everyone's needs and wants are identified:

> Successful use of the collaborating technique should end with a sound agreement.

The pushover may, however, feel uncomfortable and

seek to back out of a discussion – although they will find that hard to do in the face of such reasonableness. So again, lots of collaborative patience and (gentle) persistence will be required.

When collaborator meets collaborator

> **Everyone should be able to exchange all their tangible and emotional negotiables.**

We can say 'all' here because collaborators do not make unreasonable demands. It is possible that all parties will agree not to make an agreement.

So it's that simple?

Alas no!

> **People can change their styles many times during a single negotiation.**

So you might start out with the best of collaborating intentions and then someone upsets or frustrates you – and you react …

I remember one occasion years ago when I was co-training a workshop on negotiation. As trainers, we believe and advocate that the collaborative style is the best approach in all negotiations where both the relationship and the issues matter.

As the workshop progressed, our working relationship, as trainers, started to founder. We adjourned to the bar (a not untypical reaction amongst the trainers I know) to 'negotiate' how we could resolve the issue.

We both sought to be highly collaborative using the right words, the right voice and the right body language. After about half an hour (I just said 'do whatever you want, I'm past caring ...' Not very collaborative at all) in response to my adoption of a pushover style, my co-trainer then got angry! So:

> Even with the best of collaborative intentions, both parties can change their style at any time.

So how did we resolve the situation? We stopped talking about the issue and talked through our style of communication. I felt that my co-trainer was being 'tough'. I didn't want an argument, nor did I want to continue the discussion any further, so I became a pushover and conceded any point he raised.

Yet his perspective was that he had started and remained collaborative throughout. A key learning point evolved:

> You are only truly collaborative if the other party *believes* that you are being collaborative.

When we both understood what had happened, we were both able to resume – albeit with more care – a collaborative negotiation.

Should I be admitting to you that I got it wrong? Yes, because it's important to note that:

> Interpreting the negotiating style is never easy!

In summary

- two tough negotiators are unlikely to make progress – unless one concedes

- when a tough negotiator meets a pushover, the former is likely to get everything they need and want – and the latter precious little

- the key when a collaborator meets a tough negotiator will be who has the greater persistence

- when a pushover negotiates with another, there will either be a weak agreement or none at all – but it will be 'pleasant'

- a collaborator can encourage a pushover to achieve a sound agreement, albeit the latter might experience some discomfort

- two collaborators working together should deliver success for everyone involved – even if it's an agreement not to agree

- you are only truly collaborative if the other party

believes that you are being collaborative

- people can – and do – change their styles many times during a single negotiation
- interpreting the negotiating style is not easy.

8

Tactics

Tactics are the different strategies and activities designed to support a negotiator in achieving their success criteria. Broadly, different styles use different tactics and therefore:

> Individual tactics can be a strong indication of a negotiator's style.

However, sometimes we interpret actions as deliberate tactics when they are actually done in innocence or as a cultural 'norm'. For instance, in some cultures, arriving late would be an insult while in others it would be a cultural necessity.

If you *know* that you are being subjected to a tactic, you could ask:

> What would happen if we both used such a tactic?

They just might stop using it as a result!

Handling tactics

We have already explored the different styles of negotiating and what happens when styles come together.

So which style should we use against which tactic? Generally:

> The pushover will either ignore or succumb to tactics,
>
> The tough negotiator will respond to tactics indifferently or with another tactic.

But the collaborator response is more complex:

> Collaborators handle tactics.

Now, let's look at twelve collaborative rules to deal with tactics:

Rule 1: Parties, not opponents

> Do not refer to negotiation parties as 'sides' or 'opponents'.

It merely re-enforces (wrongly) that there is a battle to be won – you should work together to resolve the issue to be negotiated.

Rule 2: Set the ground rules

Before a negotiation actually starts, consider setting 'ground rules'. These might include timekeeping, staying respectful or how discussions will be structured.

> By stating the rules mentioned in this chapter at the start of a negotiation, you can pre-empt the potential use of many tactics.

For example: I knew I was to negotiate with someone whose goal was always to offer less than they were prepared to pay and then be 'reluctantly' forced higher in exchange for concessions from me. To alleviate this, I started the negotiation by saying:

'Can we be clear about our approach to this negotiation? Should I double what I want so you can beat me down or should I just declare what I believe to be a reasonable basis for agreement?'

His face was a picture of surprise! He then covered up his apparent awkwardness by laughing and said, 'Let's both be reasonable, shall we?' This saved much grief and time and we concluded a reasonable agreement as a result.

Rule 3: Benchmark the negotiation

This is an extension to rule 2. When you think that one or more parties intends to state unreasonable needs and wants, it can be useful to 'benchmark' the negotiation.

Benchmarking is a comparison of the similarities and differences between two situations.

Start by looking at negotiations which were based on reasonable needs and wants. Compare these to the negotiation you are currently involved in that is hindered by one or more parties making unreasonable demands. Those negotiations don't even have to be on the same subject – just have some common ground that can be compared. This comparison should provide a means of making reasonable progress.

Seek agreement that all parties should be reasonable in identifying their needs and wants.

Rule 4: Know your authority

You should not enter any negotiation unless you know exactly what your authority is (and what it isn't). State this authority up front to avoid others seeking to negotiate with someone else in your organization from whom they might think they can get a better deal.

Rule 5: Explore needs and wants, not demands

This is often referred to as position- taking or making demands.

> When faced with position taking, always focus on what interests (their needs and wants) underpin that position.

For example: 'We will not settle for less than a 10% pay increase' can be responded with: 'I hear that – can you tell me on what basis you are making that demand?'

Note, however:

> Do not repeat their position (it suggests some level of agreement), yet do seek to understand what lies behind their position.

Rule 6: Isolate strong emotions

We said (in chapter 1) that negotiations have emotional needs and wants. When you believe that strong emotions are influencing a negotiation, they must not be ignored.

> Strong emotions should be acknowledged before tangibles are negotiated.

Empathizing with the emotions that are probably felt by other parties can help to diffuse a situation. Further,

> **It helps to acknowledge your own emotions at the same time.**

Then seek to agree that everyone will put their emotions aside to ease what has to be a nonetheless challenging negotiation. However:

> **Be realistic. Emotions will still arise.**

When opening a negotiation, agree how emotions can be managed – perhaps by asking for a 'time-out' without explanation or comment from the others.

If the emotions still inhibit progress, consider introducing a mediator or arbitrator (see chapter 3).

Rule 7: Challenge sweeping statements

> **Challenge stereotyping, generalizations or stubbornness.**

For example:

Challenge 'All you people are stupid' with 'I disagree. Nor do I believe that such comments add anything to this discussion – wouldn't you agree?'

Challenge 'Your products are too expensive' by 'I believe that we are competitive – but I am happy to look at any specific examples you can give me'.

Challenge a blatant 'No' with 'What never? Surely there are circumstances when ...'

Rule 8: Ask for specific evidence

Do not allow vagueness in negotiations. If you have any reason to doubt what you are being told, ask for the evidence. For instance:

'That really surprises me. I haven't heard it before. Can you tell me where I can look that up for myself?'

This is a direct challenge. It will work for a collaborator *if* you allow the other party to side-step the challenge (if they want to) and move on to other issues.

Rule 9: Do not antagonize or insult

When you know someone is lying to you, it is so tempting to call them a liar – but don't!

No matter what is said, avoid making personal attacks.

Rule 10: Stay calm yet be persistent

I can't deny that sometimes I have wanted to lambaste someone for their total intransigence or blatant stupidity. But:

> **Stay calm no matter what happens!**

(It is perhaps a different matter when I am out of earshot!). And remember:

> **The key to successful collaboration is being persistent.**

Rule 11: Step towards agreement

This is a process by which you ask a series of logical questions which are always worded to engineer 'yes' answers. On the fourth or fifth question, you should be ready to ask the real question to which you want them to say 'yes'. (They will find it difficult to say 'no' after their sequential series of 'yes' answers).

For example, if we are faced with intransigence during a financial negotiation following a divorce, we might ask the following questions, each stimulating a 'yes' answer:

1   'Would you agree that this is a fairly emotional process?'
    Answer: Yes

2   'Would you also agree that it would be much better to get an agreement you can both sign up to rather than have the courts impose a solution?
    Answer: Yes

3 'Is it fair to say that an agreement is not feasible without understanding the perspectives from both sides?'
Answer: Yes

4 'So you have to agree that all the needs and wants need to be identified in order to move on?'
Answer: Yes

This is called a 'stepping agreement'.

> Stepping agreements are very useful for a wide range of negotiating tactics.

Rule 12: Be honest

Some people think they are convincing liars – so convincing that they actually start to believe themselves! There is, however, no substitute for honesty if all parties need to be able to look back favourably at a negotiation with the benefit of hindsight. Being honest includes:

> Saying 'no' when appropriate.

If you are asked something which is totally unacceptable, then say 'no' – waffling around a refusal suggests you will concede the point.

The rules:

So to summarize the collaborative rules:

Rule 1: Parties, not opponents

Rule 2: Set the ground rules

Rule 3: Benchmark the negotiation

Rule 4: Know your authority

Rule 5: Explore needs and wants, not demands

Rule 6: Isolate strong emotions

Rule 7: Challenge sweeping statements

Rule 8: Ask for specific evidence

Rule 9: Do not antagonize or insult

Rule 10: Stay calm yet be persistent

Rule 11: Step towards agreement

Rule 12: Be honest

There is a caveat, however, in applying these rules:

> **A collaborative negotiator will always understand and respect the culture of the other parties.**

Applying the rules

Let's now see which specific rules would help us the most in response to the tactics identified in earlier chapters.

First, let's explain the table reproduced on pages 72 and 73:

- the first column identifies which style of negotiation this tactic is *typically* used by: 'T' for

Tough, 'P' for Pushover and 'C' for Collaborator

- each tactic is abbreviated from that referred to in the chapter for the T, P or C negotiator
- the rule numbers refer to those itemized in this chapter
- the main rule that applies to a tactic is both 'ticked' and in bold type.

Using tactics

We have now explored the three typical styles with their respective tactics and what happens when two styles meet in a negotiation.

This guide advocates the collaborative style for many (but not all) negotiations, since it represents the least risky of the three styles outlined.

However, some would maintain that:

> **The riskier things are, the greater the rewards when successful.**

And

> **Your success criteria and resultant style choice will be a balance between the risks you are prepared to take with the potential benefits you might reap.**

So:

Used by:	Tactic / Rule number:	1	2	3	4	5	6	7	8	9	10	11	12
T	Dishonesty	✓	✓			✓		✓	✓	✓	✓	✓	✓
T & P	Lack of honesty		✓			✓		✓	✓	✓	✓	✓	✓
T	Withholding information/knowledge		✓			✓	✓		✓	✓	✓		
T	'I know your boss personally'				✓			✓			✓		
T	Quoting third parties			✓				✓	✓				
T	Requesting a higher authority		✓		✓								
T	Repetition of demands					✓							✓
T	Claiming reasonableness		✓	✓		✓	✓		✓		✓		
T	Refusing to listen	✓	✓	✓							✓		
T	Refusing to let others speak	✓	✓								✓		
T	Refusing to speak/silence		✓			✓						✓	
T	Moving the goalposts		✓			✓					✓	✓	✓
T	Demanding last minute concessions		✓			✓					✓	✓	✓
T	Brinkmanship, threats and bluffs	✓	✓				✓		✓		✓	✓	✓
T	Threatening to end the negotiations	✓	✓				✓		✓		✓	✓	
T	Abruptly ending negotiations	✓	✓		✓		✓				✓	✓	

Used by:	Tactic	Rule number:	1	2	3	4	5	6	7	8	9	10	11	12
P	Playing on one's naivety													✓
P	Appealing to the other's better nature			✓			✓		✓	✓		✓		
P	The sob story, the tears, the apologies, the begging			✓			✓	✓					✓	
P	Inflating the importance of anything that helps them 'save face'								✓					✓
C	Honesty and openness													
C	Seeking to identify and understand the needs and wants of all parties						✓							
C	Respect for others even when they don't agree		✓											
C	Challenging unreasonable attitude/behaviour							✓						
C	Staying calm, objective										✓			

It is now up to you to decide which style (and supporting tactics) are most appropriate for any specific negotiation.

In summary

- tactics are the strategies and activities used by a negotiator to achieve their success criteria

- different cultures might interpret (wrongly) that a tactic is being introduced

- different styles use different tactics and respond differently to their use

- the use of individual tactics can indicate a negotiator's style

- the collaborative style is advocated when dealing with tactics

- there are twelve rules to deal with tactics

- all tactics should be dealt with within the context of the parties' individual cultures

- you must decide which style (and therefore which tactics) are most appropriate for each negotiation you are about to embark on.

9

Successful negotiations

In chapter 1, we concluded that:

> A negotiation is a communication during which the parties seek to agree an exchange which delivers mutual benefit.

Words like 'agree' and 'benefit' lead us to this chapter's key message:

> Motivation, rapport and trust are key elements to a successful negotiation.

With these elements, not only can we encourage people to negotiate openly and honestly with us, but it also increases the likelihood that the outcome from our negotiation will be implemented as agreed.

Motivate to negotiate

Sometimes we need to motivate people to join a negotiation (rather than ignore a request to do so).

It is likely that any reluctance to negotiate is prompted by their preferred style (that of a pushover) and/or a lack of personal benefit from giving up their time for the necessary discussion. For instance, you want to agree with your brother and sister a means of sharing financial support for your parents (whom you have been supporting exclusively for the last year). Your brother doesn't want to get drawn in to any discussion (being a pushover) and your sister sees nothing but financial worry for herself if she offers any help.

How can you motivate them to negotiate with you?

The clues to motivation are in the emotional negotiables already identified.

So when talking about parents, nearly everyone will have some form of emotional tie: loving, being loved, respect, obligation, guilt, duty etc. And we can use this to identify their:

WIIFM? What's in it for me?

So we might encourage the family to the negotiation with:

'Mum and Dad are still very much in love and deserve

to have many years together without worrying themselves over money – which we should try and help with'. (Love, obligation).

'Mum and Dad never failed to come rushing in when we needed help – however difficult it was for them … now it's our turn'. (Guilt and managing any reluctance to get involved).

And so on.

A positive WIIFM? is to be preferred over the negative alternative:

> **Negative WIIFM?s warn of the consequences of inaction.**

'Mum and Dad will end up living on the streets for lack of money'

or

'Mum and Dad's house will start falling to bits – and so will our inheritance – unless we can help them out now financially'.

Motivating without a WIIFM?

It will be difficult to motivate people to participate and then adhere to a negotiation if there is absolutely no gain or benefit for them.

So look again for a WIIFM?

If that still fails, the only obvious alternative is to adopt a tough negotiating style, rather like the street mugger who negotiates to steal my wallet in return for not harming me. Hardly a formula for success in most of the negotiations you will be involved in!

Motivating to gain agreement

We can use the emotional negotiables to ease progress towards an agreement. We can also select a key motivator from the following:

- people are prepared to exchange (i.e. pay) more if they get the **best service**. This would also extend to organizations that have the highest reputation/ image of service.

- people can be motivated to spend more to get what they want to **meet their time-scale**

- some will agree to an exchange to **preserve or enhance a relationship**

- most of us are motivated to make an agreement when there's a **competitive price**!

- many will pay more for higher **quality**

- some would be motivated to make an agreement on the basis of **the reputation of the other party**. For instance, I might hire a lawyer who has the best success record. This might, in part, be motivated by someone wanting to **enhance their own reputation** through being associated with a highly reputable organization.

- if the next door neighbour has the latest computer technology, others may be **competitive** and want the same – or better. And potential **competition** from other parties over limited supplies will motivate a deal – that's why things are sometimes marketed as 'limited editions'.

- **innovation** can motivate an agreement. How many people do you know who want to own the latest technology before the price stabilizes at a lower level?

- **functionality** – some agreements can be secured simply by advocating that it will do, reliably, whatever it is the party wants.

- and some of us will do a deal just to have our **dreams or desires** fulfilled – however irrational and expensive it may be!

So:

> Identify what the other parties need and want and then present what you offer as fulfilling their motivations.

The customer/supplier relationship

> Don't assume that you are trapped into adopting only one style in a certain situation.

A prime example is when a supplier thinks they should be a pushover and the customer thinks they can be tough. Suppliers can be collaborative if they introduce motivational factors to secure an agreement. For example:

As one of many suppliers of widgets, you might have always been a bit of a pushover with customers and accepted whatever they were prepared to pay, afraid that if you asked for more, they would go to one of your competitors.

It is true to say that:

> If you only negotiate on one thing – price – then the only way to agree a deal is to reduce the price.

However, there are other negotiables you can introduce from the motivation factors outlined above. Focus on the motivation factor that matters most to the customer and you might even be able to increase your price.

Back to our widgets:

If the supplier discovers that the customer wants widgets delivered minutes before they are needed, any supplier who can guarantee quick delivery can probably charge a premium. This collaborative negotiation has become possible by appealing to the motivation of an otherwise dominant – or tough – party.

Rapport building

> Having a ready rapport with others will help overcome any difficulties and speed the negotiation along.

So what are the basics in establishing rapport?

- smile, offer a firm, confident handshake on meeting
- be polite and respectful throughout
- show you have prepared by knowing and responding to their cultural needs and wants
- at the negotiation's start, establish common ground outside of the field of negotiation. Perhaps a mutual sport interest or holiday destination you have both visited.
- use their buzz words. People favour certain expressions/phrases/words – using a few will encourage others to be more receptive. For instance, when negotiating to provide consultancy services, I will use some of the client's words to convince them to strike a deal – if they want 'fantastic profit', that is the phrase I will use (but sparingly).
- express understanding of their situation, needs and wants.

Rapport building is a huge subject. For other ideas on how to build rapport, ask yourself:

What has happened when you found yourself getting on really well with someone on your first meeting?

Because whatever you did, you obviously established a ready rapport.

Rapport and trust

If you can establish rapport with someone, trust should follow. And for an agreement to be implemented with ease:

> Trust is an invaluable asset.

So again, ask yourself what makes you trust others? What makes others trust you? Now apply your answers to your negotiating style and it should support your success.

In summary

- motivation, rapport and trust are key elements to a successful negotiation*
- there will be occasions when you need to motivate parties to start a negotiation
- clues as to what will motivate people to start or complete a negotiation rest within their emotional negotiables.
- package your motivating pitches as a WIIFM?: What's in it for me?
- a positive WIIFM? is preferable to a negative one
- discover what motivates others and introduce it

* For more on building rapport and trust, see the Easy Step by Step Guides to Successful Selling, and Motivating Your Staff.

into your communications

- do not assume that individuals are only motivated by one factor
- do not assume that a particular style has to be adopted for certain relationships (for instance between a customer and a supplier).
- establishing a good rapport eases progress past any difficulties and speeds the negotiation along
- if you can establish rapport with someone, trust should follow.

10

The logistics

All negotiations are subject to logistics – the timing, the means of communication and the location.

> **The logistic elements can be used tactically to support any style.**

For example, a tough negotiator can choose a bigger chair, the pushover might seek to work on their 'home ground' and the collaborative negotiator will be wise to all positive and negative attributes of the logistics – and plan accordingly.

Timing

Timing can have an enormous impact on a negotiation. If too far in advance of anyone's needs or wants, people will see little point in finding the diary space or commitment to get started. If too near a deadline, an agreement can be rushed and not thought through. The former might be preferred by the pushover (there's no pressure), the latter by the toughie (exerting lots of pressure!)

And springing a 'surprise' negotiation on someone is not a good idea either. Everyone must have adequate preparation time, even if they choose not to use it effectively.

So what would the collaborator do?

> **Agree a future timetable for discussion, setting interim and completion deadlines.**

Deadlines will focus attention and ensure that nothing is rushed at the last moment – they should be agreed before negotiations start.

And to prevent someone having to leave a negotiation when on the edge of an agreement:

> **Agree in advance how much time the parties should allow for each negotiating session.**

What other timing considerations are there?

- what would be a reasonable time for all parties to arrive at (and leave) a location, without being exhausted or perhaps jet-lagged?

- can avoidance of interruptions be promised – or should extra time be allowed for them?

- what breaks (for food and/or drinks) should be provided and for how long?
- what contingency time should be planned in case the negotiations stall? See chapter 13 for more on stalled negotiations.

Time-outs

> Successful negotiations are made with due thought as to what is being agreed.

Planning should therefore include 'time-outs' so people have the time to think and/or consult others. Time-outs should:

- be introduced in the ground rules at the start of a negotiation
- be encouraged
- be granted on request
- be of agreed duration before they are taken
- have suitable rooms available (that is, equipped with appropriate communications technology and have a high degree of privacy).

During time-outs, all parties should leave the negotiating room. This avoids undue pressure on those in time-out – 'we must hurry, the others are waiting for us'.

If telephone negotiating, time-outs can still be requested.

Calling back in ten minutes with the right response is infinitely better than an immediate wrong one!

The means of communication

> Negotiations are generally easier when undertaken face-to-face.

Face-to-face communication has less chance for misunderstandings (or more precisely, early recognition when misunderstandings may be occurring).* It is also easier to build a rapport (and therefore trust) in such situations. A caveat to this would be that:

> Face-to-face misunderstandings can still occur – not least if a party is communicating in their second language.

Not all negotiations are undertaken face-to-face. They could be done by letter or email (even 'texting'). Telephone/video conferencing could also be used. Certainly the preamble to any negotiation may take place using these means – for instance, when seeking an advance agreement on the timing issues.

Location

Assuming that the negotiation is to take place face-to-face, let's consider the attributes of a good location:

- convenient to all parties
- offer an appropriate degree of privacy
- be isolated (as much as possible) from interruption or distraction
- have appropriate seating arrangements (see below)
- be properly provisioned – be it with stationery supplies, refreshments or whatever. For large groups, this would also include name cards
- have appropriate communications technology – especially in the time-out rooms.

Seating arrangements

The tough negotiator will want a bigger chair and/or a dominant seating position (such as the head of a table) – possibly a confrontation seating plan where parties sit on opposite sides of a table.

The pushover will generally sit wherever they are told but will probably want the seat nearest the door (for a quick escape!)

The collaborator will want a more equitable layout – perhaps a round table with alike (and comfortable) chairs. If only two people are involved, they may select to work across the corner of a table – or without a table entirely.

> Negotiations can and do take place in your sitting room or an office corridor, but it should still be an appropriate choice.

Your place or mine?

The tough negotiator will want others to come to them – to which the pushovers will naturally agree.

The collaborator will select a location by its suitability and convenience. They will not be intimidated by going to someone else's place of work. In fact:

> The collaborator may deliberately choose a tough negotiator's location above all others.

Why? Simple – it panders to the ego of the tough negotiator. By going to them, the collaborator lulls them into believing they already have a success. And that success has cost the collaborator nothing. It can also be very difficult for the tough negotiator to accept failed negotiations – the tough negotiator will not want their peers to see others walking away.

Prepare the logistics

Having chosen the timing and the location:

> Organize the logistics thoroughly and in plenty of time.*

---

* The Easy Step by Step Guide to Fewer, Shorter, Better Meetings.

In summary

- the timing, the location and the means of communication are all important elements to achieving a successful negotiation

- agree interim and final deadlines to ensure there is a commitment to progress the negotiation without them being too tight to inhibit due care and consideration

- agree the time that should be set aside for each negotiating session before it starts

- time-outs are invaluable to ensure that whatever is finally agreed is right for all parties

- the best way to manage, if not avoid, the potential for misunderstandings is having a face-to-face negotiation

- misunderstandings can happen when one or more of the parties communicates in a second (rather than their first) language

- choose a location that meets the needs of the negotiation and all its parties

- determine what would be the most appropriate seating arrangements

- meeting at one party's location can be beneficial to the others

- organize the logistics thoroughly and in plenty of time.

11

A checklist for successful preparation

We can now pull together all the different strands that make up the necessary preparation for a successful negotiation.

When researching, remember that:

> There is a 'fine line' between research and spying. A collaborator favours the former and the tough negotiator, the latter.

So let's get started with a checklist of questions to which you must identify all the possible answers.

The start of all preparation

- what is this negotiation about?
- who should be party to this negotiation?

- what would motivate each party to join the negotiation?

- what deadlines are there? If none, how can a deadline be agreed (i.e. negotiated) amongst all concerned?

- what are the main tangible needs and wants of each party (including your own)?

- what is known about prior negotiations by and with the negotiators and their organizations?

What to research on the other parties

- who (specifically) will represent them?

- what are their (probable) authority levels?

- how can you build a rapport and trust with these individuals?

- what cultural issues might arise? How can/should you respond?

- what are their probable success criteria for the negotiation?

- what (do you think) will be their non-negotiables?

- what are *all* their possible tangible needs and wants – for themselves and those they represent?

Think 'big' on tangible needs and wants!
Even if you *know* you cannot meet a need or want, do not discard it at this stage.

- prioritize those needs and wants – which do you

think are most important to them? A simple approach is to give each a high, medium or low priority.

- estimate how much *you think* it will cost you to provide each of these needs and wants?
- what are their emotional needs and wants? Think about both the negotiators themselves and those they represent. This should lead to:

> **What negotiating style are they likely to adopt?**

- how might their emotions be responded to?
- what tactics might they deploy and how might you best respond?
- what would motivate them to make an agreement?
- how reasonable are their needs and wants?
- what will they do or what will happen if an agreement is not reached? This can give you a clear understanding of how powerful they might feel.

What to prepare about yourself

- who (specifically) are you representing?
- what is your authority level?
- what are your success criteria for the negotiation?
- what will you absolutely *not* negotiate on?

- what are *all* your possible tangible needs and wants – for you and those you represent? Think big! Even if you *know* they cannot meet a need or want, do not discard it at this stage.

- prioritize your needs and wants – which are of high, medium or low importance?

- estimate how much *you think* it will cost the other parties to provide each of these needs and wants.

- what emotional needs and wants do you and those you represent have? And be totally honest in answering this question:

> **What impact are these emotions likely to have on your behaviour, attitude and style?**

- how might these emotions be responded to?

- what tactics are you going to use and how might they respond?

- what is your motivation – and that of those you represent – to make an agreement?

- how reasonable are all your needs and wants? (Be honest!)

- what will you do or what will happen if an agreement is not reached?

A bottom-line?

Having a bottom-line (the minimum you would agree to in an exchange) carries significant risk:

- you might only seek that bottom-line and fail to miss an opportunity to secure much more

- if you only achieve your bottom-line, you will probably feel you 'lost' in the negotiation

- failing to meet your bottom-line would mean that you walk away from an agreement (unless you decide to take on the pushover style) – and that could be the wrong decision

- your bottom-line might be unreasonable, so an agreement becomes extremely unlikely unless you adopt a particularly tough style (with all the risk that brings).

So 'bottom-lines' are perhaps not the best strategy. Instead, consider:

What can be done if the negotiations fail?

This is the Best Alternative to a Negotiated Agreement or BATNA.

An example

One of our previous houses was valued far higher than we expected. We couldn't resist the temptation to make a considerable profit, so we put it on the market – but it didn't sell. We hardly got a single viewing.

Lesson 1: If your needs and wants are unreasonable, you may not even find someone to negotiate with.

But we emotionally wanted to move – so we substantially reduced the price to a realistic level and a potential buyer came along who was willing to negotiate a purchase, albeit at a price below what would have been our absolute minimum.

> **Lesson 2: If there's a bottom-line (on price or anything else), it might prevent an agreement being made.**

But we concentrated on our BATNA, our alternatives. We wanted to move (a very high priority, if not a non-negotiable), but we didn't have to buy any specific house – there were lots of alternatives at different prices.

> **Lesson 3: Remember there are alternatives to meet your high priority needs and wants**

So we sold at a reduced price and bought another house. Needs and wants of both parties met in a collaborative negotiation – with one exception: twenty-four hours before closing the deal, we were asked for a further price reduction. It appeared that the deal could collapse unless we conceded.

So – was this a bluff? It was certainly a tactic – but using what style? And how did we respond?

Well, our top priority tangible need (to buy the house we had by then chosen) would still be fulfilled by closing the deal even at a reduced price. But our emotional needs and wants had moved up to the top of our priorities – we wanted to move! So we changed our style (becoming pushovers) and accepted that small price reduction.

> **Lesson 4: Priorities (just like style) can change as the negotiation proceeds – especially in respect of emotions.**

So, looking back on this negotiation – would I or should I have handled it differently? On balance, I would say that while I didn't like the tactic, I was right at the time to concede it. As I said in an earlier chapter:

> **Lesson 5: Sometimes, the collaborative style is not necessarily the right approach.**

In summary

- preparation is key to a successful negotiation
- every party (including oneself) to the negotiation must be researched as part of that preparation
- think 'big' when identifying needs and wants
- determine each party's non-negotiables
- identify, prioritize and cost needs and wants that can be negotiated
- determine the level of reasonableness of the needs and wants

- consider potential motivations, history, style and tactics when undertaking your preparation

- determine what each will do if no agreement is reached

- avoid having a bottom-line but do have alternatives

- priorities – just like styles – can change as a negotiation evolves.

12

Let's negotiate!

A negotiation process

Having completed our preparation, we are now – at last – ready to negotiate! There are six stages to a successful negotiation: opening, discovery, exploring, trading, closing and getting it in writing.

Now we will look at these in more detail.

Stage 1: Opening a negotiation

First impressions count – so make them count in your favour with a positive welcome, a smile and firm handshake (as culturally appropriate). Ensure everyone is introduced (including whom they represent).

Briefly, state the subject you are there to negotiate – without giving any indication as to the possible outcome. So it would be:

> *Appropriate*: 'We are here to discuss the possible supply of widgets'.
>
> *Inappropriate*: 'We are here to secure the best possible price for widgets'.

Remind people of the benefits that would accrue to them if the negotiation is successful. This can be particularly useful in counter-balancing any negative emotions. If there are high emotions in the room, acknowledge them:

'I believe we should appreciate the emotions that are likely to be present in discussing this issue. I would recommend that we seek to put these to one side as much as possible, while respecting the reality that they may well surface at some point.'

Agree the ground rules, time-outs and potentially, the preferred negotiation style:

> If collaboration is your chosen style, declare it and seek agreement that all parties will also collaborate.

Note: the ground rules should give an indication of what 'collaborate' means, a brief summation might help. Perhaps:

> 'To work together on the problem to see how successful we can be at meeting the needs and wants of everyone represented here.'

But:

> If you have determined to be tough or a
> pushover, don't announce it!

To conclude the introductory stage, outline the proposed structure for the rest of the negotiation. So we might say:

'Can we agree to a staged approach – first finding out all the issues, needs and wants, then their relative importance, before considering as many different ways as we can to achieve an acceptable outcome in arriving at the best possible solution.'

For team negotiations, it is advisable for each party to nominate a lead spokesperson. The role of an independent chairperson might be useful for large groups.

If this is not the first negotiating session, re-state the progress to date and the agreed ground rules. Before proceeding, secure agreement to this introduction (checking whether or not any of that should be reconsidered).

Secure agreement, and move on to the next phase.

Stage 2: Discovery of Needs

Now we check out your research, specifically in respect of the parties' tangible and emotional negotiables, the non-negotiables and the parties' success criteria.

> Remember: People are likely to take a 'position' (their tangible wants). To move forward collaboratively, concentrate on what has made them take that position.

So there are lots of questions to be asked here: 'What do you need?' will start you off (although perhaps it is a bit abrupt). This is known as an **'open'** question – one designed to 'open up' the conversation.

Then expand on their answers with **'specific'** questions: 'What exactly do you mean by ...?', 'What specific quality do you need?' etc.

Keep asking questions until you have identified all the pertinent information.

If you don't understand their answers, re-phrase the question or say you don't understand. Use **checking or summarizing** questions to be certain that you have understood: 'If I have understood you correctly, you specifically need ... Have I summed this up accurately?'*

End this part of the negotiation by asking a **closed** question (one that invites a single word answer: a 'Yes' or 'No'): 'Is there anything else to be negotiated?'

So, in the discovery phase:

> Ask a sequence of questions: open, specific, checking, summarizing and then closed.

And to get the process moving:

> Give a little information, ask for some in return.
>
> Don't be fearful of being the first to speak.

But all this is useless, whatever style of negotiation you use, unless you

> **Listen carefully to the answers!**

And this includes listening carefully for what is *not* said or what might be an incomplete or evasive answer. For instance: 'I think that's all I need' or 'That's all for now'. Follow up such responses to discover their underlying meaning.

If you are adopting a collaborative style:

> You must also reveal all your tangible and emotional negotiables, your non-negotiables and your success criteria in this phase.

Since you will be so well prepared, you could perhaps just read through your list. But it would be better (i.e. less intimidating and less smug) to allow others to ask questions to elicit the information from you.*

---

*See the Step by Step Guides to Communicating With More Confidence, and Successful Selling.

You should not move on in the negotiation until everyone's information has been shared to prevent later surprises – unless, that is, you are being a tough negotiator!

There is a possibility that in the light of what you have listened to, you think you should change your BATNA (or bottom-line if you insist on having one). Such changes should only be made with considerable thought.

> **Changing your BATNA or bottom-line requires the negotiation to start anew.**

Stage 3: Exploring needs and wants

This phase is to:

> **Determine the relative priority of the others' needs, wants and success criteria.**

The concept under-pinning this phase is that what you might regard as of little or no value, could be vital to the other party. So unless you 'explore' effectively, you might 'give it away', when they would be prepared to exchange something substantial in return. A good negotiator will 'trade' everything – nothing is given without an exchange.

And to introduce it:

> Ensure that all the parties clearly understand that this is an exploration only and not offering an agreement.

And, as before, if collaborative:

> You need to reveal your relative priorities.

We use another type of question in this phase – **'conditional'** or **'what if'** questions. For example:

'**What if** you paid 30 days earlier than usual and in return we were to give you a 10% discount – how would that appeal?'

This question should identify which is more important to the other party – price or cash flow?

By constantly exploring different combinations, the others' priorities should be established. (This is true even if the parties haven't worked out their priorities in advance).

Some words/expressions you might use include:

'Possibly ... perhaps ... supposing ... how about ... just an idea/suggestion ... in theory ... without committing ourselves ...'

Once this stage is complete:

> Call a time-out to assess all the gathered information and consider what might be the best possible outcome of the negotiation.

Stage 4: Trading

Now it's time to 'trade': 'I will do ... and in return you do ... – are we agreed?'

> **Never give anything for free (even if valueless to you). Everything should be 'traded'.**

Be persistent in asking for that which matters most to you, summarize frequently and as each part is mutually agreed, write it down – signal it as a success and then move onto the next point.

> **If you need to reject a possible trade, do so clearly and succinctly.**
>
> **If you hesitate, they will persist.**

However, rejecting a trade is more likely to be acceptable if you offer a counter-trade. Persist with this stage until the best possible outcome has been identified.

Stage 5: Close the deal

When everything has been successfully traded, we must close the deal:

> **'I'll leave it with you then' or 'I'll give you a call' are *not* closings.**

Some closing techniques:

- summarize the benefits of what is proposed (the WIIFM?s) and ask for the deal

- offer one final concession on the proviso that the deal is agreed *now*. (Allowing a delayed agreement here usually results in the concession becoming part of the accepted package in future discussions. Make it clear that the concession will be withdrawn unless agreement is made immediately.

- offer a choice between two alternative outcomes (when either will result in a successful negotiation). It's hard for people to say 'no' to both!

- as a tough negotiator, you could exploit a party's fear of not having a deal: 'Can you afford not to do this?'

- as a pushover, you can always beg! (But who's to say whether or not it will work?)

Determining when to close a negotiation will usually be self-evident. However, look out for closing signals from others that they are ready to make an agreement. For example: if someone says I will buy it on your terms, don't ask them to wait until you have completed all the earlier phases of a negotiation!

One tactic used in negotiation is the 'Silent Response'! To illustrate:

You ask a seller for their cheapest price. They answer – and you remain silent. If the seller is anxious for the sale they may well reduce the price further to close the deal.

Similarly, if you are asked to close the deal and give the 'Silent Response' it might prompt a last-minute concession being offered to tie the deal up.

Such silent responses work best with doubtful or frowning expressions.

Stage 6: Get it in writing

No, I'm not expecting you to sign an agreement with your friends about where you will be going for a night out!

However, writing down an agreement in full can avoid disputes or misunderstandings later on.

> Ideally, each party will write down the agreement and then cross-check it before anyone leaves the negotiation.

And this has an added bonus:

> When someone writes something for themselves, their commitment to 'stick to it' is higher than if someone wrote it for them.

And success will only be achieved if the parties are committed to implementing the agreement.

Some agreements have to be subject to contract or perhaps signed-off by others. Governments, for instance, might sign treaties subject to affirmation (or not) in a referendum. So be it – but it must still be written down when first agreed.

Walking away from a deal

There will be times when you should walk away from a negotiation – the parties agree not to agree.

This should not cause discomfort for any party if:

- They mean it (i.e. that it is not merely a tactic).
- They are 100% sure that there can be no agreement to meet the parties' success criteria.
- Each party has already determined how else they will seek to secure their needs, wants and success criteria.

However:

> **Walking away from an agreement might be the best option, yet it can take courage.**

Pushovers would rarely walk away for fear of upsetting the other parties and the perception that they have wasted the others' time.

Tough negotiators might walk away as a tactic. If there is a genuine desire to walk away, they may find it easy (because they don't care what people think of them) or difficult (because it raises doubts among their peers about their skills in negotiating). So a tough negotiator's ease of walking is strongly influenced by their emotions.

So what of our collaborators? These people seek agreement by everyone that the best option is to walk away – and then do so.

In summary

- there are six stages to a successful negotiation

- open the negotiation confidently and by agreeing the basis for proceeding

- discovering the needs, wants and success criteria of all parties must be completed before moving on in the negotiation

- good negotiation is about asking lots of questions and listening carefully to the answers

- identify the relative priorities among all the information you have discovered without 'doing the deal'

- after perhaps a time-out, start 'trading' and do not give anything for nothing. Clearly refuse the unacceptable

- when the best possible outcome has been identified, close the deal and put it in writing

- there will be times when the best agreement between the parties is to walk away from the negotiation.

13

Stalled negotiations

There will be times when a negotiation stalls and we need strategies to move the discussions forward. What happens next?

Summarize

The easiest way to move forward is go back! Summarize the last point of agreement and seek a (different) way forward from there.

State the agreed process

Sometimes stalling can occur because the parties have lost track – re-state the approach that was agreed at the outset and try again.

Ask for their help

If you believe that a negotiation is stalling, ask the

other parties to help you address it.

Common ground

Discuss the common ground or common success criteria, perhaps by re-emphasizing why the parties were entering a negotiation in the first place (their WIIFM?s).

Conflicting vs. complimentary ground

Conflicting ground (i.e. conflicting success criteria) can cause a negotiation to stall. For instance in a customer and supplier negotiation, one wants to buy at the cheapest possible price, the other to sell at the highest. However, the same scenario can look at the complimentary ground to move things along – each party wants to make profit from the exchange.

Presenting complimentary rather than conflicting information will help the parties to seek a mutually beneficial way forward.

Separate the people, the issues and solutions

Stalling can occur because one party does not want to accept another's idea – however good it might be.

If you think this is the reason for the difficulty, write everyone's ideas on, for instance, a whiteboard. By mixing up everyone's ideas, the ownership attached to each should diminish.

Unreasonable intransigence

This can be a tactic and warrants challenging. However, it may be appropriate to adjourn to give time for reflection and/or consultation with the people represented by the negotiating parties.

Refusing a great deal

Yes, it happens. You believe the perfect deal has been worked out and yet one or more parties can't bring themselves to agree.

This suggests that not all of that party's needs and wants have been adequately responded to, so return to the discovery phase to check your information. This will also be necessary if the 'goalposts' appear to have moved.

It costs nothing ...

An apology costs nothing – even when you see no reason to offer one. But it can diffuse a stalemate and allow the parties to move on.

Give them trophies

Encourage parties to believe they are being really successful, perhaps with a little exaggeration. Such awarding of 'trophies' minimizes the likelihood of a failed agreement because, after receiving trophies, few of us would like to have to give them up!

High tensions

If tensions – and tempers – rise, call a time-out for reflection.

Off the record

In exceptional circumstances, and with great care, you could consider off-the-record chats to seek to identify why a negotiation has stalled. There's a reality here, however:

> Rarely does off-the-record stay that way.
>
> It has a habit of coming out at a later stage.

So whatever you say in such circumstances, be prepared to have to stand by it later.

Introduce an arbitrator or mediator

See chapter 3.

Change the range of negotiables

One of the options available is to change the parameters within which the negotiation is taking place. For instance:

- if a company cannot agree the sale price of a piece of equipment, try leasing it instead, perhaps with the involvement of a third party who could buy the equipment and then lease it on

- if the family cannot agree (because of different needs) on what to do for the weekend, perhaps they should consider what to do over the next three weekends so that everyone gets what they need.

Change the negotiators

The negotiators could be changed – especially if there is a breakdown in rapport and/or trust. This should be perhaps something of a last resort since any new negotiator would have to start the process afresh.

Trial agreements

Negotiations can stall because there is some form of doubt by one or more of the parties. Perhaps they doubt whether time-scales or quality goals can be met.

A trial agreement could be reached here – agree to a small part of the exchange and, subject to a satisfactory outcome, the whole deal will automatically be agreed. However, it is vital to:

> Closely define what is meant by a 'satisfactory outcome'
>
> If this is at all vague, the full agreement may never be implemented.

In summary

- there will be times when negotiations stall and specific strategies should be used to overcome whatever its cause might be

- if there is doubt, return to the discovery phase to check information.

14

So how have you done?

Upon completion of a negotiation – and that includes agreeing to walk away from one – assess:

> How complete and accurate was my preparation?
>
> What might be done differently in the future?

And on the negotiation itself:

> What worked well and what didn't?
>
> What should *you* have known in advance, but didn't?
>
> How should it have been different?

Plus crucially:

> **Was the agreement implemented exactly as agreed? If not, why?**

So how did 'they' do?

Assess what you believe to be the other parties' perspective on the negotiation and its' outcome. You could even ask them!

However:

> **Beware: Some negotiators would take delight in telling you they would have been happy to exchange more!**

Don't let such a response put you off asking the question. But neither should it condemn what you otherwise thought was a success. After all – if you didn't work to a bottom-line, you would have exchanged more as well.

Learn for the future

As with all reviews, their purpose is very specific:

> **What can make your negotiations even more successful in the future?**

Enjoy it

One final comment – successful negotiating can be and should be immensely satisfying for everyone concerned. So enjoy it!